I0493694

1st Year Essentials

THE SIMPLE DIY GUIDE FOR
NEW SMALL BUSINESS OWNERS

NATASHA RILEY-NOAH

Published in the United States of America

First Edition, 2013 (Audio version available here: http://tinyurl.com/ppsuujv)

Lagniappe Logic Publishing

403 West Grand Pkwy South Suite F-301

Katy, Texas 77494

www.natasharileynoah.com – Downloadable Planner Templates available here free

About 1ˢᵗ Year Essentials

The 1ˢᵗ Year Essentials line of entrepreneurial products offers our small business community only what will be essential to helping you manage every major aspect of your small business. You will save lots of time, stay organized, compliant and profitable and be more productive by using the tools within.

You will be surprised at the power a few handy notes can have on the effectiveness and profitability of your business and maintaining your sanity.

That there is lots of information on how to run a small business out there is an understatement. But the information can make your head swim and a lot of it is just information, not actionable items you can use weekly, monthly, quarterly and annually to keep your business running without overwhelming you with extra fluff.

Unlike those formal business plans business owners usually never read after they spend months cranking one out, lots of the information out there is in the form of regurgitated SBA (Small Business Administration) tips and advice that lots of people know of but never implement, this will be something that you actually use!

By the way - one of the only business planning tools out there that I consider to be actually helpful to real world folks like us is called LivePlan (go to their website if you want a closer look: http://www.liveplan.com/)

You may have a well thought out, well formatted business plan and it may be beautifully researched and designed, but implementation is either implausible or difficult because most of that stuff repeats itself throughout or you may get lost in technicalities to take any actual steps to make your business better.

Sure, if you are looking for funding and the method you are using to run your business requires such a business plan, it is good to have one on file. But some of us have more than enough proof and experience in life to know that these types of plans are rarely used to actually guide daily decisions and operations.

Wouldn't it be better to also have something on your desk that you can refer to and read easily, in plain English?

With 1st Year Essentials™ on hand, you will have the necessary and immediately helpful steps right at your fingertips. Additionally, knowing exactly what you need and how to clearly inquire about things when you do begin working with legal and financial professionals saves you time, money and prevents lots of errors.

Getting clear is the key to being good to your business and it being good to you.

I wish I would have had a guide like this by my side for my first entrepreneurial go-round years ago! Important things would not have slipped through the cracks and I would have known the right questions to ask of lawyers and accountants.

I didn't know what I didn't know...you know? It would have actually saved me about $18,000 plus in operational setup costs in my first year!

But I digress...

Getting back to brass tacks:

If you want to really maximize this thing, use it at least weekly. Squeeze out every helpful idea you can while following the required operational checklists to keep your organization on track. Though this may not carry every single possibility required to operate every conceivable business type out there, it is highly useful for anyone going it alone and just starting to get things straight.

Almost all popular small business resources, books and programs, seminars and workshops with gurus, coaching and consultation phone calls that I have spent time and money on over the past 15 years is all condensed here, modernized, simplified and straight-to-the-point for you.

You won't have to spend thousands like I did to get this information and years of time organizing it all to have it handy. You won't have to make thousands of dollars worth of mistakes that I made with my businesses.

Picking this guide up and perusing it for an hour with your Friday morning coffee is one weekly habit that will help you and your business stay on point for profit.

Who is this book for?

Well, I am assuming that you have an established business or you have been freelancing for some time now and you now need to get more compliant and need a simple organizational system to do so quickly.

You may be a solo-entrepreneur who is at the cusp of hiring help, but you want a workflow with built in check and balances first so that you can manage properly.

You are not a person needing to be coaxed into actually setting up your LLC or S-corp because you have already done so or you know you must and are currently looking to do so.

You are a contractor whose main accounting procedure consists of writing up estimates on napkins and throwing your supply store receipt behind the seat of your truck, but you want bigger jobs and need to prepare you books for a CPA to get a bond.

You are a neighborhood restaurant owner and you are so busy fixing the dishwasher and trying to hold on to good wait staff, you don't have time to think about paperwork so it is in your closet at home overflowing in boxes. You feel profitable because there is money left over in your bank account, but you want to be sure so you can make the best business decisions you can with suppliers, employees and location.

You are a self-employed insurance agent that is so busy with her kids and home life, her clients follow up calls are suddenly getting pushed further and further back on the calendar and that 'to be filed' pile has grown to hide half the wall in her quaint little home office. You know you need an assistant, but not sure if you can afford one.

See…the people who will benefit most from reading this little quickie are real folks, just like my clients and my husband and I.

They are the true independents. They design their lives to be different…on purpose.

They self study and self medicate! They dropped out of college because the business started growing. Besides, the only 4.0 they had while they were there was their blood alcohol level anyway! (Saw a cool t-shirt that said that once…awesome!)

They are often misunderstood for taking risks others around them would never dare to take, so their friends and family don't really 'get it' when they are having a bad day.

They are the people who hack their way into self employment because they are skilled at what they do or they are naturally good at sales.

They need to turn their office chaos into harmonious order to grow and be more profitable and in order to continue feeding their families.

And finally, they employ over 80% of the people looking for work in this country – and a big reason that the US economy regains any momentum after a recession.

Yes, that's us.

And we need to make sure we have our act together because a lot rides on our shoulders. We are the doers not the theory pushers. We need it simple, straight-to-the-point and actionable…and if we need help, we need it yesterday.

That is the spirit of this book and the energy behind anything I do for small business owners.

I am not trying to offend any MBAs or CPAs or lawyers with writing my little DIY guides. I have worked with many and many are still my dearest friends and affiliates helping when I need their expertise.

But honestly, most would probably laugh anyway at my lack of sophistication and my horribly improper usage of the words 'who' and 'whom' (I never could get that right!), so this little book is not for them or people looking for MBAs, CPAs or strict and academia-heavy legalese. There are many books out there for you already – have fun!

This book is meant to be functional and based on years and years of experience operating small businesses and assisting entrepreneurs in the real world – the everyday, nitty-gritty stuff that keeps us compliant and able to see a growing bottom line through do-it-yourself means.

In other words, this book is for the rest of us.

Now, I am not saying that you can't get good information here if you have not started your business yet. As a matter of fact, this would be excellent for anyone in the planning stages of their business idea, because it helps them know exactly what will be required to stay organized and have a smooth as possible workflow.

It can also help a person whose business has been open more than a year already but they just want to get a better handle on what they are worth or make some changes in how they operate.

Whatever your stage or situation, this book can help you achieve and maintain order in your business.

If you do not see anything here that actually helps you after trying it out, email me: nat@natasharileynoah.com and let me know today.

I am very confident I am in the information I have gathered, simply because it is from real world experience.

Also, the fact that I have helped many other small business owners who were overwhelmed get caught up with their books, tax reporting and corporate paperwork and helped them have a streamlined workflow that is compliant for their industry makes me know that this will work for you. But only if you do what is recommended in this book each week, month, quarter and year will it truly make a big difference for you and your business..

But you have got to DO these things to SEE them work for you.

So please, try them first. Fill in the planners and checklists with specific items you need done regularly or items that you need to delegate to the right person or service.

Implement the suggestions, email me and ask questions, bring your business just one level up from where it is now and see the profitable difference and the time and stress it will save you to do this stuff.

You will be glad you did.

Here is the layout:

1. **Motivation** – This is an essential. Even if you are solo, you still need to motivate yourself regularly to keep the flame burning for your business. Really simple and helpful.

2. **Marketing** – This is the marketing focus for all of the members of your organization. It includes identity training and USPs, social and traditional media, client contact management. In other words, telling everybody about what you've got.

3. **Management -** This section outlines the regular operational duties, daily and weekly organizational tasks, and some analytics will influence day to day operations. Manage your business daily or quickly go crazy. We list a few more essential to dos specific to all the data in the main areas you always need to stay on top of.

4. **Money** – This section is obviously for controlling cash flow and financials at-a-glance. Here is where you refer your bookkeeper and CPA every service interval. They will appreciate you bringing in organized and easy to understand material and you will save time and money using their services after this work is done. So keep this section especially straight. This section will also include to dos for:

    a. **Money In** – Cash, credit and debit card swiping, checks and any other way you accept money from clients for your products and/or services (and this does include tips!)

    b. **Money Out** – Bills and any expenses related specifically to your business operations, production and serving clients; and

    c. **Tax Time** – Do these things every February and you will never have to rush again

5. **Modernizing** – This little section gives up to date rules on globalization, green efforts, corporate social responsibility and in-house policies that are progressive, keeping you above customer expectations in your business and contributing to your community. Plan how you will make your impact here. Here, we also explain the biggest reason WHY going paperless is becoming a very basic way to handle your essential

paperwork and some regular management tasks like **Disaster Proofing–** Step into the future and find the easiest way to backup on the cloud for you.

6. **Momentum** – This concluding section is for long term planning ideas. Things like scalability or sustainability and model clarity, and notes from your professional advisory team or board would go well here. The **Important Docs** needed for momentum should be maintained well and the standard for most small business owners is listed here, along with what to keep on file, paper or electronic, for at least 5 years (5 years minimum for most industries)

7. **The Summary will include:**

   a. **Resources** – Official information, government links, and professional organizations that are designed to help small businesses succeed.

   b. **Sample Planners** – Use however you wish and of course my very own

   c. **Recommended Reading** – In my humble opinion, these are must-haves for every new entrepreneur - whether in your library, in you desk, in your Kindle or iPad, audio versions on your mp3 player.

Let's get cracking!

Disclosures – in plain English

☐ Don't try to avoid it. You will DEFINITELY need a practicing attorney, Certified Public Accountant, financial planner, insurance agent and/or risk adviser, psychiatrist, physical therapist, housekeeper, au pair, yoga instructor, and a damn good bartender to run your business like a pro!

Seriously though, please get professional advice only from legal, medical, and financial professionals. We know lots of stuff that can help you, but this checklist cannot completely replace all types of professional advice. You agree that you will retain your own professional for all of your specific business and personal needs. Please do so. QuickBooks, legal services memberships and good old Uncle Mo are good for some things, but not all.

☐ If I could, I would write down every possible thing that you might need in one place. But honestly, no one will be able to cover every entrepreneurial possibility for you in one checklist, outline, seminar, workshop, book or program. So please do not consider this all inclusive, because nothing ever is.

☐ Naturally, you hold us harmless for your results and realize that the recommendations here are merely suggestions based on good proof of it working well for others.

You are not required to do what anyone says and your choices are your own. Remember, we all go into business at our own risk, like the community swimming pool! I may make commission on some, not all, of these recommendations.

☐ The items and tips presented here are subject to constant changes and updates. This world is changing by the nanosecond and any of the internet links and recommendations I provide today can immediately change.

The IRS may change its rules, your state or province can change its laws, your county or parish may update their small business licensing requirements, and authors can change the site where their books are found and so on. Please be sure to check up on everything I say with your regional administrators, municipal laws and rules, industry regulations, favorite publishers and authors or whatever have you.

☐ Before you speak to anyone about your business ideas, make sure you get your copyright, patent or trademark applications and paperwork completed. I am not saying that you should turn into 'that guy' that pulls out a non-disclosure contract at dinner before you start talking about your business to friends, but use good judgment and be careful with whom you speak if this is a concern for you.

These types of applications are detailed but fairly easy to comprehend – it's not that difficult to figure out how to do on your own. If you find it difficult when you start to look them over, do more research and/or hire competent, professional, experienced help.

☐ I get straight to the point in this little eBook, so it is small. This was intended at first to be sort of a 'rough-and-dirty' checklist for extremely busy people and turned into just a bit more than that. Please share the information you find helpful with our entrepreneurial kindred and spread the love.

If you need more customization or more detailed information, email me at: Nat@NatashaRileyNoah.com. I am here for you and would love to connect you to whatever you need to succeed!

Motivation

Okay, I promise I won't get too woo-woo here, but I would be remiss if this was not where we started. Motivation is a huge deal and you are kidding yourself if you think it is not as important as other items on this list.

Motivating yourself and your team to give your best to your business is definitely easier on some days than on others. Never neglect this essential piece of the puzzle.

Let's go over a few things you can do to keep yourself and/or your team motivated.

Use this when things are especially pressure-filled, when you are having trouble focusing on your work, or when you notice that lots of time has passed and you have not managed it well.

Energy Assessments:

Check lighting, colors and clutter in your work environment and try to make things as bright, cheerful and Zen as possible to promote clarity and ease.

If someone around you is in a bad mood, do not try cheering them up (per se) because this can drain your energy and take your focus from your work. Bring them a cup of tea, water, soda, and give them an immediate reason to say thank you and be grateful in the moment.

Don't say a word, just give them something small and thoughtful.

If in 30 minutes this random act of kindness does not lighten the mood, suggest that they get fresh air for 15 minutes and come back. When sharing space, this is so extremely important, so take this information to heart and use it whenever you have to.

Check yourself and your breathing when you start to work fast and get frantic or after dealing with something that made you nervous or frustrated. Stop, stretch and breathe for 30 seconds to circulate your blood flow and move oxygen through your body.

This works! If unable to focus, repeat once more.

Still stressed? Then take a 15 minute break and walk outside if possible. Come back with fresh-brain so you can focus like a laser and get more things done.

Culture Check:

Easy to influence when you are your own boss. Make certain that your workspace screams aspects of who you really are. Things around you that speak your truth will dominate the mood and tone of your work environment and help you feel centered and useful, which gives you energy to get things done.

If your employees have habits or traits that you find a little annoying, but they are great at their jobs and you love having them on your team, block aspects of those traits from your daily view.

You would not believe how much time you spend in your head judging people and not putting your whole head into your work.

Philosophy/Mission/Vision Reminders:

These three terms mean essentially the same thing. If you think of them as the same thing, your business will reflect the truest part of who you really are. Keep these in sync with what you do for your customers, employees and your business overall and with what you truly believe is valuable and meaningful about you and your world.

It is also good to take the time, usually about 5 minutes or so when you feel pressure, to write down one sentence that answers this one simple question:

Why do you feel good about your business?

When you answer this question honestly, here is what comes out:

'I feel good about my business because it does (blank) for a person, which helps them to (blank). My employees and I feel the same way and they love (doing, making, selling, showing people how to-blank) just as much as I do. (wrap it all up like a third grader essay reading)…and that is why I think my business is great…thank you!'

Look at that answer. This is the structure of any business philosophy, mission statement, or business vision.

Plain and simple, right?

You can split hairs on semantics about what to call it and the perfect title of it until the sky turns red. But again, it is essentially always going to be why you feel good about what you are doing everyday in one or three sentences.

Personal Processing (mental checks for owners):

Based on personality and beliefs, we all have a certain way that we process the stress in our lives. Some people meditate like a Buddhist monk and chant in a dark room on a pillow, sitting in lotus position.

Some are yoga addicts and never miss class and others pray and sing inspirational songs along with powerful choirs and loud music in their house or car.

Lots of us fall in between somewhere, and just might add a happy hour at our favorite bar or a quick jog or bike ride at sunset to help us relax and assess our day.

And if you are a nerd like me, you might even have one of the hundreds of your favorite audio programs playing in your ears as you cook or when you let the dog walk you.

Whatever method of personal mental processing you use to deal with your daily realities, my advice is to do it in the morning every day, for an hour. Wake up earlier if you must.

If you do it daily before the stress hits, it will serve as a preemptive strike against the inevitable energy drain that comes with being an entrepreneur.

Group Activities (for camaraderie, harmony and unity):

If you have a team, these are quite valuable for pressure packed days and weeks. Prayer (hey, lots of musicians do it before performing, and if your industry and size allows you to do this without offending anyone – go for it!), reading, volunteering, music, cleaning, exercise, in-house activities and events, rewards and recognition are just some examples of what a team can do together to help process stressful team duties.

Here are a few more ideas for team energy lifts -

- ☐ Music or motivational audio or video you listen to before a meeting
- ☐ Pep talk or inspirational story in a coach-like voice from the fearless leader
- ☐ Cheering for each other during a tough assignment or laughing at a you tube short
- ☐ Game or team activity with gifts or awards
- ☐ Food to share – fruit basket, coffee or smoothie gallons, pizza, pastries, candy, etc
- ☐ Volunteering during a holiday to feed the homeless as a team or help build a home (annual activity)

Marketing

Ideas on marketing your business abound on the Internet. It can be overwhelming when certain people preach about how they made thousands of dollars overnight by sending out an email or tweeting.

Social media usage and email blasts are going to make people notice you and your business. This is true. But, a lot of these people who make thousands of dollars a night on the Internet have been blogging and growing their list and presence for a few years.

What does this mean?

It means those thousands of dollars are not typical results for anyone blasting an email or tweeting about their business.

A relationship was developed with that person's list follower way before they finally decided to buy during their business product launch. Powerful though it may be, the Internet is not in and of itself the easy way to business riches without a super strategy.

Purely You

The first thing to spend time on with your staff (and to study if you work alone) is identity training and Unique Selling Proposition purity. Training yourself and your staff to fully understand how you want your business to be identified is so important; it is almost inexcusable if this is not taken seriously.

I had the most trouble with this starting out and I find that whenever I expand my business services, I have trouble with it all over again because of the change in my Unique Selling Proposition or USP.

Your USP has to be clear, quick and sound so that people get it and know if they want you. With most local or regional small businesses that are started by solo entrepreneurs with a certain skill set or product, it is pretty easy because they rely on their title and specialization to be their USP.

Such as:

I am an insurance agent. I sell Health Insurance.

I am a contractor. I build family homes in Mid-City and New Orleans East.

I own a small bar in the Irish Channel Neighborhood.

I am a Mary Kay consultant.

A really good USP takes it a step further, but usually won't feel natural at first to people who have leaned on statements like those above to answer the question:

What do you do?

Slightly better USPs will have a little punch and sound something like:

I help self-employed people avoid horrendous medical bills.

I help create great neighborhoods for families in the city I love.

I give people a cool place to hangout close to home.

I make women feel confident.

Finding the right USP for you and finding one that feels right takes time. Don't stress out over it. Here is how your business can immediately have USP purity:

A. Use the old fashioned mainstays until you get a testimonial from a happy client.

B. Then, use what they say when they referred you to their friend – it will be a winner.

C. Repeat it as your pure USP. It will feel right because it won't feel like this false thing you came up with to fit in at a small business marketing seminar. It will be what someone else said about you. You will just be repeating it.

(You keep it pure by making certain it really does reflect what you business focuses on with its products and services and it changes when your business changes.)

Once you have locked down on a good USP, train your employees to use it and program your contracted help to know that this is what your business is all about.

That is how you become known for what you do and how you position yourself in your market. Just keep getting better and better at your business and your brand will position itself higher and higher on your industry grid.

This is definitely one of those areas where information abounds on the web. Social Media this…tweet that…it's pretty much everywhere ad nauseam. Here, we will hit the basics and just let you feel out the media outlets you feel most comfortable with to regularly start using.

Please note: both on and offline marketing are extremely important for all types of small business. Some businesses will do more in one type of media than another due to the industry or the setup of their particular operations, how they interact with customers, etc.

But even those businesses who do not use the internet to make sales still need a website for customers to locate and know a little something about their product and service offers.

That said, if you have been resistant, and I say this with the utmost love and respect, get over it and just do it, even if it is just a little!

Questions make very powerful Facebook posts and Twitter tweets. They usually illicit some type of response if you are strategic and use it for real marketing. Tell people in your target market what you do and how good you are at it. List testimonials and encourage them with little bribes, I.e. discount coupons for referrals.

Questions targeted to your market's problems are great for service businesses. Try not to overuse questions though. Every other time you use social media, try also using facts that you want your customers to know as posts and tweets.

Post and tweet at least weekly and try to make monthly offers, coupons, or discounts for re-tweets, shared posts and collected email addresses from interested prospects.

Traditional media are still viable ways to connect with your local, regional client base. Radio, TV, newspapers (if any are still left running in your city), flyers, mailings, and anything you have been doing that actually has at least a 60 day return on the investment of money and time.

If an entire 6 months has passed by using these means and you have not seen a return, kill it. Don't keep doing things that don't work just because it is what you've always done.

Client contact management

I am assuming that you already have a website or blog, but in case you do not, get one. Even a quick little 3 pager is better than nothing. List it with basic information, pictures, location and owner/staff info or whatever information you would put on any flyer.

Once you have your site up, and for those who already do, there are several super simple ways to start collecting names, email addresses and other customer info.

My favorites are:

- Mail Chimp – email list manager and a great marketing campaign program
- Wufoo – simple form maker (no technological experience required)
- AWeber – one of the best email list manager and pop up form creators around

  Good old Microsoft Excel and Microsoft Access work great as well if you are an owner that likes to handle this yourself from the beginning to build the list from scratch. Just look for a contact management template under 'New' and start adding your info.

Shoeboxed.com is a service that can collect your business cards and create a functional database for you. All you have to do is stuff them all in an envelope and send them off. 3 days after they get them…boom…a database is created just for your business.

Done! (How awesome is that)

Shoeboxed does a whole lot more than just scan business cards – they are a business partner of mine and I will give you more info on them later.

These are simple ways to start gathering all of your customers' info in one place. With the economy changing and the global marketplace expanding, you always have to be ready to take your customers info wherever your business may go.

Changes happen, and being flexible can help your business ride through any of them. Keep your relationships strong with your customers – at all times.

Relationships are the key to effective marketing.

When you think about marketing your business, you should first consider what it will take to begin developing relationships with the people who would benefit the most from your offerings.

Selling is not the goal.

Relationships are the goal.

Here are some ideas to get you going to develop and maintain your vital relationships: Offline and online and of course, in-house:

- ☐ Offline – Branding & Logos, Biz Identity Tasks & Promotion, Traditional media outlets, scheduling – press kits, Special Event planning, Networking with complementary industries, Referral boosters, offers, and gifts for customer appreciation

Online, you can do much of the same as offline – Social Media Usage Schedule/Digital Strategy

- ☐ In-house – Customer Contacts, holidays, birthdays, testimonials, reviews, referrals, sales letters, newsletters, special reports, printed materials and client correspondence

It is your job as the business owner to come up with the first idea. Then allow your team member to enhance or embellish based on actual experiences with your customer base and prospects. Always kick off the discussion and let your team wow you with implementation ideas after you start them off.

Marketing is simple – don't complicate it. Block out the noise and go for what you know works for you and your business.

Management

Daily operational tasks that help your business actually function falls under this very broad category and this section can literally go on for ages – which is why it is a degree plan at most universities.

First, let's streamline here to focus on the main areas most small businesses need to laser in on within the daily operations. Then we will talk a little more about a few other important details that should be included after these are handled.

The main areas are:

- ☐ Employees or Contract Hiring Decisions and Planning
- ☐ Sales Tracking and Analytics Reviewing
- ☐ Customer Service and Issue Resolution

Remember: When you are a solo entrepreneur, you must be careful to never, ever, ever let this section dominate your time. Always plan for help, even long before you find any and constantly write down the things needing to be done (or record them on your voice recorder on your phone if you have to – then send the mp3 file to a transcriptionist for often only $1 per minute or sometimes even less)

A pattern will emerge through this process that will show you plainly over a 30 day period what exact tasks needs to be delegated – and this is the person/skill set you hire first. Once you have over 10 per week of tasks needing to be done from this emerging list of items, it is time to hire someone. Part time or virtual assistance services first. Then as you grow, full time and/or regular B2B services from companies that provide what you need.

Employees or Contract Hiring Decisions and Planning

It is the ultimate balancing act, but if you cannot hire physical staff right away, you can get help through business to business services (B2B), certain software, some easy to follow templates and worksheets or by outsourcing certain tasks to freelancers or hiring virtual assistants.

Delegation is sometimes scary for new business owners. But remember the beauty about being the boss: you get to choose who helps you. The trick to this is always picking the person for the task who loves to do what you need done. If they love it, they will do it well and accountability is almost a non-issue. But all tasks delegated should always have deadlines and metrics to track.

Reviewing employees and contracted hires will swallow some time out of your week, but this is a must-do item, because it directly and immediately affects your bottom line. This is a management item that you must take the time to do, and I would have you do this monthly.

It should only take an hour or two if you have a weekly tracking system in place for delegation of duties and a way to see if those duties were done.

Review the work that meant the most to production and sales that month and review the activities of the person you hired.

Did they meet your expectations? Are they valuable to have at your business? Great…move on to your next to do item.

If anything was lacking, take five minutes to discuss it with the person, and be sure to keep it to only one item and only five minutes. The results of only 2-3 months of this process will tell you if they are beneficial to your company.

Sales Tracking and Analytics Reviewing

Deadlines for task completion and sales goals help to keep you on track for your goals. Set your goals and glance at them as often as you need to so that they are on your mind, but do not obsess over goal setting.

Here is a tip to get straight to the point when goal setting without having to buy or download special software and complicated worksheets:

What do you want and when do you want it by?

That was your five thousand dollar per ticket goal setting workshop in a nutshell!

Make a list of these goals every week, month and quarter and just maintain that list.

Simple…

Sales tracking can be done by simply counting the products you sold by unit and by category if you sell several products. This means you will have to maintain some inventory analytics, either by delegating the counting of inventory weekly or daily to an employee or having your inventory measures automated with software or through a service.

Sales goals tracking for a service business involves counting how much service was provided or how many new clients were gained by looking at the fees, commissions or number of new clients collected that month against a baseline goal, which just helps your business break even, and a profit goal, which is self explanatory.

Thinking like your customers

Surveys suck! There…I said it!

I hate developing them. I hate taking them. (Please know that I am not telling you to hate them or never use them. If you believe in surveys, then, by all means…)

Why do I feel so strongly?

Because no matter what any statistician or green Marketing graduate tries to beat into me, I know people are NEVER honest with those things unless they have recently – and I mean within a matter of 7 days or so – had a significantly bad experience or a significantly good experience and want the management of a company with which they had this experience to know about it…specifically.

That is about the only time these stupid things have any weight in my eyes, but these times are so rare, wasting precious time creating regular surveys makes no sense to me.

How many times have you told some poor customer service worker on the phone you would give them high marks on the survey that would follow that may have, oh I don't know, slightly exaggerated their actual performance?

(Ok, Natasha, tell us how you really feel about surveys!)

Feedback – customer care reviews – blah, blah, blah…all platitudes and nonsense. And I know this will polarize me from the people who want to beta test and split test and test all of the tests…the price I pay for being me, I guess. Paying attention to the types of issues we resolve for our clients will give us the information that we really need to help our clients not have repeating negative experiences.

Here is how we doers do it – think of that old adage 'look for forgiveness instead of permission'…

Look at your refunds!

Reviewing the reasons for refunds give you poignant information you can actually use to make your business better today.

- ☐ Take a 90 day period.
- ☐ List how many refunds you had, noting the time and employees on duty, especially if the employee your clients interacted with was you. Note the reasons for the refunds.
- ☐ Adjust your system or work-flow for any items that came up over 3 times within this time period or with the same employee.

Another idea – FAQs!

Consider the questions you are constantly asked by your customer base and write them down. Then decide if you want to implement improvements to your business based on the items you see fit from that list.

I have, within my business, a system we have patented call Client MindSwap™ , where we use support tickets, refunds, FAQs and other specifics directly from our client's experience with us to make further developments to our services and operations.

I did this with my current businesses because certain complaints were a real problem with one of my prior businesses. I left too much in the hands of employees and certain contractors I hired and I did not stay at the helm of my clients' experience and on top of the things that really mattered. It makes a real difference when you do and the proof is in the profit!

Simple! 1-2-3

To my fellow business owners – don't complicate your life thinking you have to do all of this research and testing a certain way to be successful. This way actually works quite well. Use it and save you and your staff time and stress.

Other areas of management and operations that will require the owner's attention are areas that require taking one step back from frontline activities, considering the structural controls on your business and the workflow. These are things that will create momentum in your business and will be discussed later in another section, aptly named 'Momentum'.

That's how you cut to the chase. Moving on...

Operations Tracking

Here is an area that will require discipline. The more tips and checklists you keep in front of you every day, the easier the note-taking will become over time. Lots of this information can be a short, sweet and simple note, a Microsoft Word document or a text document. Use whatever you feel most comfortable using now for record keeping.

If you handwrite these items, scan the handwritten pages into your computer and file them in a computer document file marked 'Business Records'. You may also have these typed for you by someone on www.fiverr.com , a great freelancing service site to get very simple things done for you and your business starting at only five bucks!

Significant changes to structure or operations of your business

When you decide to change from sole proprietor to an official LLC or S-corporation, you must make notes regarding your decision to do so. Keep this little note entitled 'Minutes' or 'Board Meeting' (yes, you can have a board meeting all by yourself!) with the date on it, right next to the receipt and contract for services that you purchase to incorporate and organize.

When ever you decide to change vendors from which you purchase regular supplies, your business location or mode (meaning if you decide to become a mobile business as well as provide services in a fixed location), keep these notes as 'Minutes' or 'Board Meeting' clipped to whatever change expenses you incur, i.e., new lease, website design and related online marketing expenses, new mobile phone services, new equipment you will use and the case you will safely transport them in, new vendor terms if you purchase supplies wholesale or on credit, etc.

Vehicle Mileage, Maintenance and Repairs that gets you to and from your clients or vendors

Always note your mileage daily or weekly when you drive to clients to give them service and when you drive to vendors to get supplies in your little handy mileage notebook you keep in the glove box. Currently, the IRS (2011) gives 51¢ - 55.5¢ per business mile in allowable vehicle deductions. Remember, you will either benefit more from recording mileage or recording expenses. The IRS will not count both mileage and expenses within the same tax year for your allowable deductions. So it is best for the first couple of years that you record this information to keep track of both mileage and expenses so that your tax preparer can help you use the best option at the end of the year.

If you ever change your vehicle to one with an alternative fuel or energy source, like a hybrid car or electric car, make notes on all servicing done. There are huge tax breaks for this currently in the tax code that you want to take advantage of for as long as they exist.

Maintenance does include detailing and washing receipts, oil changes and tune ups and new tires and other such services to keep your car running well. Keep note if you pay for these services cash.

Repairs are definitely worth keeping track of, because these deductions can help the numbers add up quick, which can help you lower your taxes tremendously. Again, remember to keep notes if you pay for these items cash.

Money

Wouldn't you like to have control over your cash flow and know how to have your financials to the point where you can produce reports and know your financial status at-a-glance? You can, you know…

Here is where you can handle the duties yourself or delegate these tasks your bookkeeper every service interval. Your service providers, i.e. bookkeeper, CPA, Tax Preparer, Financial Advisor, etc. will appreciate you bringing in organized and easy to understand material and you will save time and money with your CPA during tax time if the financial statements are completed ahead of time.

You are the owner and you should want to have some idea of how the money is flowing. It is also a must that you write out your actual financial goals, before receiving the business' first income dime if at all possible.

You want to think about the money rules you want to play by in advance before jumping into the game. This gives you great beginning momentum. There are services that can help create a strategy that includes proven technologies that easily maintain your books.

You would want to make sure that extremely qualified, experienced personnel accustomed to servicing businesses just like yours are handling your books, so that you a highly responsive mediator between you and your CPA .

This saves you so much time and hassle, leaving you free to handle your day to day business.

And consider a situation where you stay out of the loop and have no idea what's going on with the money and all of the potential for fraud. Starting with just a simple log can initiate an internal controls system, with which you can develop a segregation of duties with trusted employees and business services contractors as you grow.

It is not as time consuming and difficult as you may think. This is vital to your business survival, so you really should take the time to keep this section especially straight.

Help for your numbers -

Be strategic with your bookkeeping and tax planning as you operate from day to day. QuickBooks or Wave Accounting are by far 2 of the best to use to get this part of your business life in proper order. Set aside the typical business plan craziness, complete with suggested and fully researched supposed-to-be's on projections in Excel that tend to make any newbie's eyes cross!

Let's simplify!

☐ Income tracking: How does money come into your business? Cash register,

PayPal, Square or Go Payment Mobile Card swipe, checks in the mail? Keep a simple log of all income sources, amounts and dates until you are able to integrate a software system to capture your income as it comes in.

☐ Expense tracking: When do you pay your bills? How do you pay your employees and contractors? At the very least, you should keep a written list of all bills, the amounts and when they are paid. Even a checkbook register would be helpful if it is kept up well as you go. Just a note – always pay your contractors and employees with checks, cashier's checks or money orders. This way you can properly track your payroll expenses and deduct them with all other applicable expenses.

Also, there is sometimes confusion for some small business owners on the definition between an employee and a contractor. It is very important that you know the difference and treat each accordingly, because according to IRS codes and labor laws, once you start to treat a contractor like an employee, you will owe those back taxes if they were not paid.

• Employees – you call the shots, i.e. their hours of works, you provide their work tools and you can get purchase health and/or worker's compensation insurance for them, and you pay taxes for each of them each pay period and provide them with a net check, forwarding their tax portion each pay period, resulting in a W-2 for them at year's end (which you provide)

• Independent Contractor – both parties agree on terms, i.e. the person really works for themselves and they are aware that they are in business for themselves as a freelancer, they are on their own as it concerns all insurance, you pay them a gross amount with no taxes deducted, they are aware that they pay their own taxes, and if you hit the IRS threshold of purchased services from them, it results in a 1099 at year's end, which you provide.

☐ Other possible deductions, receipts, statements: Using a company like Shoeboxed.com really comes in handy! Imagine dumping all of your receipts and statements to vendors, confirmation printouts , etc. in an envelope and within a few days having them all imaged, so that you can organize them and never have to worry about ink run off, losing copies and missing out on valuable deductions. (yes, digital copies are acceptable to the IRS – see Publication 552 on the IRS website)

☐ Financial Statements: Profitability checkups made easy, with the owner in the driver's seat everyday – isn't that the way it should be? Unfortunately, lots of business owners are already so overworked, they think only a CPA has the capability to show them their own numbers. But as long as you took care of the income and expense tracking listed in the steps above, you will be able to run your reports anytime you want at the push of a button.

How's that for easy?

And how great would it feel to get your yearly statements and organized receipt copies with a PDF or Excel report to your CPA during the first week of January?

Awesome, right?

Now, if you are a small business owner and you have a backlogged accounting project staring you in the face and overdue tax reporting needing completion, you face the possibility of even more delays in tax reporting, which means more penalties added to your final tax bills…not to mention the stress of having to do it all hanging overhead!

Stressed out business owners…not good.

Use this information to start tackling your backlog, or get a service to help. (See Resources at the end for more.)

Remember, there are solutions that easily integrate bookkeeping entries and reconciling with financial reporting, scanned document organization and customizing your QuickBooks accounts and lists to work for you like a little bookkeeping clerk-robot!

Most importantly, if you hire a service, they can provide the training and follow-up support afterward, which ensures that you can stay on track or catch up quickly whenever bookkeeping needs to be done from then on and produce your own reports at the touch of a button whenever you need...for instance, like at the end of the current year when your CPA comes a knocking for reports at tax time!

Money In

How are you getting paid from your clients? Keeping track of these numbers will help you make better business decisions and help you plan for tax season a whole lot better. Your categories and accounts, whether in your accounting software, in an Excel spreadsheet, or a handwritten journal, need to be customized for your business specifics.

Make sure however you are handling your bookkeeping, your system actually works well for you, systemizing your entries and journaling flow for financial reports so that your end of the year statements can be done within minutes for tax time.

Sales and Gross Receipts

- **Credit/Debit Card** payment confirmations, transaction reports and/or statements from your Merchant Account (This is the account a business owner gets from a bank or merchant services company allowing them to accept cards for payment) – if you are using PayPal Mobile, Square or Go Payment, these reports can be run anytime and saved on your computer – in a file you should clearly mark "Revenue"

- **Cash** (be very careful) – If you have a retailer cash register, this will be much easier – you will be able to run a total (z-tape) for your daily receipts. Some registers even let you export directly to QuickBooks if setup correctly.
  If you only use cash in your business periodically, keep a small log book that can fit in your pocket and write the day and date on the top of the sheets that you will use that day, with a numbered list on each sheet of who paid you (at lease a first name with last initial, full name best) and how much.

- **Checks** are good paper trails – before bringing them to the bank and making your deposit, make a copy by taking a quick picture of it with your phone and email that photo from your phone to your inbox, so that you can save your copies in your computer (delete these from your phone afterward).

E-check services are also available from Intuit, the Company that owns QuickBooks and Go Payment and other merchant service companies. This service allows you to process checks online with your clients over the phone.

Remember that it really will matter how much income you are regularly proving over time. When it is time to buy a home, get a loan, expand your business with your credit, remain in a good standing with the IRS and your state and so forth, it will help you tremendously that you kept track of things accurately. Make your income/revenue tracking a high priority.

Money Out

There are regular personal bills and business expenses that need to be recorded, which could mean extra cash to you come tax time. Remember, each time you think it is okay to handle something for your business with cash without recording it, you may just be giving up money to the government that you don't have to!

The short lists below are an excellent start to form better tracking habits.

Bills that may be deductible

Personal bills you would want to keep track of as you pay them are: Health insurance premium bills, medical bills, auto insurance bills, rent or mortgage, phone bills, utility bills, internet service bills and credit card billing statements that have business related purchases on them.

Remember, the IRS wants to see the bill and your payment of the bill by receipt or a paid statement clearly marked 'PAID'. These receipts and clearly marked paid statements should be scanned or saved in a file marked "Tax Planning documents" for the current year.

Expenses specifically for your business

Wages or commissions to your employees or people/companies you subcontract and any benefit you pay for in their behalf, payroll taxes that represent the employer's share

Start up costs, including computer equipment, furniture, items for your office (even if in your home…no, especially if in your home! Think "Home Office Deductibles".), rent - if you are leasing space, and all other expenses associated with your leased space, like utility deposits, security deposits, cleaning fees, improvements, etc.

Business insurance, permit fees, licensing fees and renewals, bonds, accounting & bookkeeping fees, bank charges to your business accounts

Postage, business cards and other printed promotional materials, office supplies, ads, supplies you buy from vendors needed to perform your services or make your products, snacks/coffee/magazines for clients, small tools, uniforms

Rental/Lease payments, equipment, utilities and telephone at business address that you pay for

Travel expenses whether a mobile business or when you have business related occurrences including lodging and meals, car rentals, taxis, plane/train fares,

Other business related expenses such as gifts or entertainment for clients or employees/subcontractors, trade show/convention expenses, professional dues, publications, books, education & workshops directly related to how you operate.

Tax Time

Because of your diligent note taking and record keeping every week, month and quarter, your tax return responsibilities will be a breeze!

Whether you do the monthly bookkeeping yourself, or you decided to save yourself the time and stress having bookkeeping, tax planning and document organizing services at least quarterly, these things must be done so that you plan FOR your taxes and don't just allow tax time HAPPEN to you!

If you take care of everything else above and follow these few tips below, you will save money and time and reduce tax time chaos.

Collect the following from your records

Prior Year Tax Return

Current tax year bank account/credit card statement copies

Money In, Money Out and Data Tracking section items

Send these copies safely and securely to your tax preparer

All items you collected above, plus

Monthly bookkeeping records and the two most important reports:

Balance Sheet

Profit & Loss

And that's it!

See how easy tax time can be when you put in a little effort every week? Very few people actually are this organized, but since you are proactive enough to read this, you won't be one of those typical people, will you?

That's because you're awesome-er than they are!

Modernizing

Is your business as up to date as it needs to be? If not, you could be stressing yourself out over small sales numbers for no good reason.

Why not capture the business that could come into your door passively?

Setup up a good system, such as a sound website, and let it work for you just like it was another employee – but the miracle kind, that works 24 hours a day, 7 days a week!

Two main things to remember while modernizing your business and your work flow:

One -

Your web presence, which would include your operational processes for servicing customers, if you will be doing so electronically, web design and enhancements so that you look as sharp as you can, and again, social media implementation.

And two -

Going 'greener' and then even going 'blue' (or in the 'cloud' as the kids say), which involves not only your own efforts in waste reduction but also telecommuting and outsourcing security policies and tasks and of course, disaster proofing your business as much as you can.

I am going to assume that if you are reading this far into this section, you are not necessarily afraid of getting hip to the globalization trends of all types of businesses everywhere with regard to this topic.

Even businesses that never thought they would have a need for a website (because maybe they are a little local service shop and always felt justified in never giving in to this whole 'Internet' thing) have started understanding the real purpose in modernizing in this way. It's to be where your customers are and to keep reminding them that yes, you are just around the corner if they need you.

You have to appreciate the fact that staying as modern as you can gives you much more presence in front of your potential market, which can give you more potential sales. You are going to need way more money to maintain your business in its first few years than you ever plan (usually 25% or more than you originally anticipate), so you might as well plan to market every angle of your products and services to raise that revenue as much as possible!

Web Presence

How you operate

How do you serve your customers? Are you a stationary business where your customers come to your address for your products or services?

Some local service businesses were in the mindset that an Internet presence was not as important as other branding efforts. But that mindset quickly changed when their competitors started swallowing up business because of online specials, coupons and awesome benefits that web positioning can give your little local shop. Maybe they didn't see the benefits before, but I am sure anyone can see them now!

Or are you a mobile business? If you will be doing business on the run, you might as well start keeping up with the 'Joneses' and know how to use what they use. Become familiar with the companies below and their offerings so that you are good to go, on the go.

I am giving you company names that I have used and loved in the past. These are not the only available companies for the listed services, as you may well know, and I am not saying that you must only use these people. Feel free to Google to your heart is content and use whomever you choose.

- Mobile card payments (those little merchant swipe tools you can hook into your phone or tablet): Square - squareup.com and Intuit Go Payment (and of course PayPal)
- Magnet Car Signs: Vistaprint and Usigns.com
- Office physical address, conference rooms as needed and mail forwarding: Opus and Regus
- Data storage: Amazon S3, SmartVault and Cloud 9
- Logo and Web Design: Logoworks, Wordpress and Intuit Homestead Websites

- Business cards and any other printed materials: Moo.com

- Packaging for products: Uline.com

- Customer Support Desk services: ZenDesk

- Other services you will need done by someone when you do not have the time: Elance or fiverr.com

- Accounting on the go, compatible with mobile merchant systems: Freshbooks (for invoicing), QuickBooks, and Wave Accounting

- Email marketing and database: MailChimp, Aweber or you can just use Excel and Microsoft Access (Google search for a sales database template)

Web design

Design can be a double edged sword for new entrepreneurs.

One the one hand, you definitely need to put time and effort into polishing your site and making it look as professional as it possibly can. "Perception is reality", as they say (I honestly forget who.) If you have what the young folks call 'website shame' and your website looks like 1995 in 2013, enhancements should be made so that you look as sharp as you can.

On the other hand, some people think that if they don't have $10,000 or more for the best designer to have the latest of everything on their site, they hold up the works and don't do any at all. Perfectionism and being lazy about shopping around can make your business suffer in sales. Don't do this to yourself. Find yourself a strong, modern looking template, or look around at other sites in your industry that get lots of traffic and go to the footer to see if they advertise their web designer.   Then contact the guy or gal for a quote.

Get the rates and portfolio examples of three designers and give yourself 24 hours to pick one. If you want to try your hand at developing your own site, here are some really cool template centers (2013) that have modern looking templates you can play around with to get started. These just happened to be my favorites and I am technologically challenged:

- Wix.com

- Intuit websites

- Moonfruit

- BaseKit

- And of course - good ole WordPress (which you can turn on after purchasing a domain name and hosting from GoDaddy) I am assuming you know what a domain name and what hosting is already if you are going to attempt designing your own website. If you don't know what a domain name is and you still want to do everything yourself, get a little bit of training first with one of the companies above by using one of their tutorials to walk you through the entire process from the beginning (domains and subdomains) to the end (publishing and going live). It may take you a weekend, but you will learn a lot.

Remember, do not allow yourself to get caught in the paralysis of analysis. Limit yourself to three and pick one in 24 hours. You can always upgrade and change things later if you want.

Using Social Media for Presence Purposes

Before we discussed a little (very little on purpose) about social media usage for marketing. Branding through social media will keep your business name in front of people in a very similar way.

I am going to attempt splitting an atom right here and give you my take on marketing versus branding. (I know I am going to get some flack for this definition attempt, but here I go. Besides, they are pretty similar concepts anyway.)

Marketing would be like using your business FaceBook page to send and reply to wall comments to tell your target market what your business actually does, such as listing your menu specials or offer discounts and deadlines, information on new services, and so forth. FaceBook pages are built based on category, so you have to put what your business does or produces and your page is usually seen and liked by people looking for that particular product or service. This group, that 'likes' you, is your target market.

Branding would be letting the public, that's the entire public, know who you are, and what you and your business stand for. For instance, using a billboard to show your logo and tell the community you and your staff donated to the local homeless shelter this Thanksgiving because you believe in strong community involvement, this type of thing would be branding (in my horribly, un-academic opinion…wait, is that a word?) Letting the world know who and where you are, letting everybody know that ABC Incorporated actually exists, that's branding.

I hope that help split those two ideas up a little for you, but let's not spend all day pining over semantics.

The point is this -

If you are just starting out, the public needs to know you exist and your target market, your actual prospects, need to know what you do and how well you do it. Using Social Media on a weekly basis, with just 3 channels for 10 minutes each, can help you accomplish both of these very important tasks.

As stated before, try the big three first, like Twitter, Facebook and Linked In (if you are a service) or Instagram or Pinterest (if you sell products) to start. Expand as you go.

Going Green and Blue

Paper, paper, paper…some people swear that having those hard copy files within reach is better for everyone. I know I use to be a person who said that often and I was petrified of anything I needed but could not regularly 'see'. But I eventually transitioned to making everything virtual in my business and now, I wouldn't have a business any other way!

There will always be some paper. In a tax preparation business that I own, we are required to have all client data for 5 years and that is an IRS rule that I cannot get around.

But, this does not mean that I have to have all 5 years of client data, and my own corporate data, and the mail all around me everyday. I would be sinking in paper! You can't be as efficient as the next guy trying to work that way, even if you know where everything is.

Trust me, the next guy these days is faster, leaner and greener than you. So don't kid yourself.

If you remain inundated in paper world with no transitional efforts to a paperless existence, you will only hurt your business. The prospect will always pick the guy who can press the button and get it instead of the guy that has to go searching and comeback a day later with it.

In my businesses, especially with the services I provide that are regulated, I do keep my paper. I just keep it away from my immediate office area, under secure lock and key, organized to the max and compliant to every rule I must adhere to. And I can press the button and get it just as fast as my fastest competition. How?

Shoeboxed.com!

(I thought I mentioned them already, but in case I didn't...)

This super awesome scanning company gives you the option to have things scanned and shredded or scanned and sent right back to you. Cool, right? So, for all items that I need back, when they come back to me, I file them by last name or company name and have them all securely stored under lock and key at my neighborhood document storage facility.

If you are just starting out, you may be able to designate a closet in your home as your locked storage (don't forget to add that lock if you work in regulated industries like mine).

Going completely paperless can keep your bills organized in one place and helps create printable vendor and payable lists for convenience for bill paying time and for when you need to compare prices, shop vendors, etc. It also helps you to create monthly, quarterly, and annual totals easily for financial statements and reports regardless of your accounting system. At my business, scanning always comes with all of our small business services and helps to make my clients disaster proof, helps them reference deductible items for taxes more easily and, if they feel so inclined, my system indexes every item they need to keep track of digitally.

Now, doesn't it seem logical that this type of system can help me as well as my clients? We can be compliant, competitive, secure and also, disaster proof all because we decided just to adopt this one concept of modernization - good ole scanning!

And if you are a small business owner currently buried in paper, this approach can help you finally get rid of backlog stress and paper overwhelm! Try a NeatDesk on for size. That is how I got my act together! I am confident that you can succeed in getting all of that paper mess tackled if you pick something to just try.

Going 'greener' and getting your data securely in the 'cloud' simply makes the best business sense not just for your sake, but also for the sake of your clients if any type of unforeseen disaster were to happen (God forbid…knock on wood). Taking these steps can help in waste reduction as well, if you shred and recycle your bits along the way.

You should impose upon yourself and enforce with your team a few firm telecommuting and outsourcing security policies so that your clients feel that you have gone above and beyond to protect their data.

Simple things like, locking the computer with a password requirement for everyone's screen savers, requiring that everyone turn in a log of their virus scans weekly so that you know it has actually been done, backing up all of the business data files on a secure cloud file and changing passwords when people leave the team are a few quick rules that make a great safe start.

NO system exists that protects from every type of possible danger. Floods, fires, hurricanes, employee theft, identity theft, misplacing important items and other crazy mishaps may happen, but because you organize yourself well with a system and have things backed up and purged regularly, you can handle things that need to be done more quickly.

It has been proven that people who have an organized system can catch thieves faster and recover much faster from disasters. {These few tasks below and more are provided in <u>Pro Unum's Annual Services</u>.}

Hard copy or CD-ROM system

Keep all hard copies of your Important Docs in a fire/water proof safe in an upper floor closet in your home or another safe spot of your choosing that you can get to easily but is hidden from visitors eyes. Also, keep your corporate kit in it as well as any other documents that would be needed to verify you or your business identification

Scan all Important Docs to CD-R (burn files of the scans onto the CD-R with your CD-Burning program on your computer) and keep the disc in the safe. Bring the disc with you when you visit with your accounting or legal team, when you travel for business and need to print copies to handle transactions, or if you evacuate your home or office location in an emergency. Jump drives are getting larger (more capacity) but are tricky for folks who lose things easily, so choose your medium wisely.

Backup on the 'cloud' services

Corporate documents that the owner will always need to remain compliant, life and medical insurance policies for the owner and key management (most recent), emergency contact lists for disaster planning, password lists, also:

All current financial reports, tax file and recent bookkeeping reports

All initial and amended corporate bylaws, articles and certificates

Business plans and projection (most recent copy)

Employee files

Payroll records

Momentum

And what can be said about the momentum of any small business…a lot depends on Business Model Clarity. All throughout this little guide, I have mentioned different types of scenarios that may or may not apply to you while describing these first year essential concepts. But being crystal clear about the type of business you own should naturally be step number one in planning.

Lets consider the main business models that most entrepreneurs choose from, just for a quick overview. Of these model types, one, two or all three may apply to your business. Remember, even if your business model is blended, one of these usually remains your dominant source of profit and thus your dominant function.

Method Models – Your business is selling a service, which is your special method of doing something that your customer needs done – solving a problem, enhancing the client's life somehow, or providing ease or simplification to a process. Examples would be a plumber, an insurance agency, an event planner or a barber.

Manufacturing Models – Your business makes something and sells your created product to the customer. Small Businesses popular in this category right now (2013) are food trucks, which is sort of a blend of Method and Manufacturing, a 'cupcakery' or bakery, or a furniture craftsman.

Merchant Models – Your business buys products and resells them with a profit margin, which your business keeps. This is also a model used for commission based businesses selling products or services that another company provides, but you may distribute to the public for them for a commission or cut of the sale. Examples here would be a boutique or even an Avon representative.

Now, let's do a little momentum planning so that once you are in business, you can have a chance at staying in business. And who knows, maybe you will even have some profit!

Planning for your Model - the simple way

The owner is the only one that can spearhead long term planning because you are the only one that really knows the ultimate goals of the business. All are involved in the momentum of the company, but the owners and partners are the leaders and they tell everyone else where the company is headed. Planning and writing out a business plan does not have to be overly complicated. But certain styles of business plans go best with certain types of small businesses and I will share my opinion with you here.

(Hey, did anyone else notice how I wrote the section on business plans near the end of this guidebook? That was on purpose! Doing all of the other items is what it takes to know you have a viable business for the market you intend to approach. The formal business plan writing is something DIYers like myself do AFTER I have tested things out a little, so that I know about the realities of my business idea before I position myself to ask for money from the bank! Now, back to main matters…)

Here is what you should focus on as it regards essential planning styles for each small business model we are considering. I will try my best not to bore you:

Method Model Planning – Your business is selling a service, so a strategic, long term plan that changes and grows right along with you works best. Strategic in that you prove within your plan that you are willing to adapt your services according to beta-tests and feedback from your client base and your target market. Long term considerations should be in this plan for, at the very least, five years at a time, because you want to be a trusted business and resource for people who come to depend on your services.

This builds Business Character, or your reputation, with your market.

The important thing with this model is being strategic and knowing:

If your service is any better than your competition and if so, how exactly?

Can you plan to scale, meaning train others this special skill of serving that makes your business great, to grow your business (and trademark or service mark of course)?

Over a five year period, will robots replace you or your team and if so, have you planned to keep the business going with the part of your service only a human can do or will you be working along with the robots?

Now, you will have to get a bit crafty to plan ahead as best as you can for some of this, but you might as well start thinking about these matters now. It would not profit you and your team to only consider this type of stuff after in the second year when the robotic calvary replaced your housecleaning staff. Only later after you shut down your operation and layoff a happy team of people who became friends of yours do you realize, you could have integrated allergy consulting, feng shui and drapery mending the way your great grandma used to do for the governors mansion in the 1800s.

That would be a shame. A darn shame.

So, if you have a service, be strategic and think long term if you offer something great! It would be shameful if your business became a statistic for lack of just one more strategy.

Manufacturing Model Planning – Your business sells products that you make yourself. You are some kind of innovating, genius, inventor person that had this great creation that everyone loves to death! Good for you…now let's plan this out further with a real, deal, formal business plan (and a lawyer and patent agent if needed), because you may really need these if things take off.

Be prepared.

Start working on your formal plan with the first 90 days of seeing sales quickly and consecutively progress or the first few months as you are working hard to keep up when you stop and say to yourself, 'Wow, I think I really have something people are responding to. This is happening faster than I expected!'

If you said that last piece, especially, you may need help with a bigger operation sooner rather than later due to demand.

This means that having a formal business plan with language the SBA can understand is best (here is where that MBA friend comes in handy dandy!) The language and technical mumbo-jumbo within a formal business plan is necessary for bank loans and investors to be happy seeing what you have and it will also:

Be in the format that investors and lending institutions expect and require ahead of time, making you look proactive and prepared.

Include details of how money is spent, which is usually what they really want to see first.

Contain some very astute market research that is essential for product sales and product business model sustainability, because you will not survive not knowing where to sell your goods.

If you invented this great thing that sells like hot cakes, get that formal business plan done asap!

Merchant Model Planning– You are a retailer, meaning you buy things wholesale, mark them up and resell them. Or you could be an affiliate or selling a multi-level marketed product that you didn't make, but gosh darn it, you believe in the product so much, you can't wait to hit the ground running! The thing with this type of business is, well…be careful and plan for YOUR future.

Here is what I mean:

Sometimes, people who go into business for themselves this way can lean a little too much on the plans of others - the original manufacturer of the products you sell who happens to make them in Korea, the franchiser who created the package you purchased or the Regional Super Dee Duper Director of Sales of your wonderful 'whozit' - these people may be giving you an idea for a plan based on THEIR expectations of their products.

You need to make YOUR OWN plan (capitalization on purpose).
Why?

Well, let's say six months in, you decide that you want to sell other things. You need to protect your standing with your valuable database. This database of prospects and clients now know you as a merchant because you have been hitting the pavement so hard, so you need to harness this power. The power of the well-liked merchant can help you sell almost anything to a viable prospect. And if word gets out that the 'whozit' made someone sick, you, the well-liked merchant, can sell a new 'whatzit' to your same viable prospect.

They are still buying because of YOU, not the particular 'whozit'.
Do you see my point here?

It is imperative that your business plan, even if in this case it is just a small, simple year by year mini business plan, includes all of the ways that you will be able to earn money in the industry that you will be well-liked for in the market you will approach.

So, if you sell purple mini dresses from your online boutique made from a manufacturer in Korea and that factory shuts down, your customers will not mind much if you decide to 'upgrade your inventory' and start offering purple mini skirts instead and could probably care less that this new manufacturer is from another country. They are buying because you became their 'go to' person in women's fashion and because they like the way YOU do business.

It is important to remember that even a short term, industry focused business plan can do wonders for your new self-employed life. Using even this type of mini-plan for your merchant model venture will benefit you, so that you don't have to fold just because someone else does.

Need more straightforward business plan writing help that won't break your brain? Look to LivePlan.com because they are by far the best for any kind of business plan development. You can change your plan, enhance your plan and see how all of your changes affected your original ideas more easily with this type of plan-as-you-go system. They are, in my humble opinion, the greatest business planning system or software around for those of us who are do-it-yourselfers!

Legal Stuff

And last, but absolutely not least, this section is your quick and dirty CYA checklist (CYA = cover your butt) for your business operational legal matters like disclaimers and policies, liabilities, managing risks and corporate level compliance for your business.

All legal corporate duties, such as satisfaction and refund policies, or service terms, disclaimers and disclosures in an ideal world should all be written by lawyers specifically for what you do.

I am not a lawyer and I would never tell anyone to go this route DIY, well not completely.

You should have some idea of what you want to say to protect yourself in risky situations with customers and at least draft out some primitive idea of what your attorney needs to include in these policies. There are books and templates that you can use to get started on your drafts before bringing them to your lawyer to fine tune. I personally like NOLO as a resource because lawyers wrote their material and they try their best to make it easy to digest and categorize their books for main industries.

(For those of you who are 'positive thinker' types, please remember to use your meditation pillows before and after these tasks and drink your harmony tea!)

Being an insurance agent for 15 years has taught me a lot about why small business owners get sued. You can be sued for looking at someone funny, coffee being too hot, a floor being a little too freshly cleaned. You name it!

You will never, ever be able to protect yourself, your team and your business from every single possibility out there. But if you do not consider this important, honestly, you should not do business in any of the Americas (try a country where they are all happy Buddhists, you may have better luck!)

And definitely get the right type of insurance coverage specifically for your business risks, I.e. Business Insurance. Don't try to piggyback off of your homeowners policy by default, because you may have a rude awakening when your claim is denied and a client cleans your financial clock!

Side note: Review your risks (no really review them) yearly before renewing your policy so that as you grow, your exposures stay covered and you can sleep at night knowing you have the right insurance policy in place for your products and services. Also, you will notice that I do not go over business structure types here and how to pick your entity, such as S-Corps, LLCs, etc. I believe that this is a matter best left to a professional service. I provide entity formation services and more extensive information on how to choose for yourself can be found on Pro Unum's website.

In industries that are heavily regulated, such as food service, insurance and tax preparation and anything to do with children and the elderly, make sure to have your best practices internal audits regularly.

What in blazes is that?

Well, it basically means you should check up on yourself quarterly the way an outside regulator would so that you can spot areas in your business where you need to tighten ship and enhance processes with clients or quality assurance methods. It is sort of like being your own policeman before the police come. If you do this, you and your team will have the comfort of knowing when the compliance police are knocking on the door, everything is in line and on point.

Let 'em in!

Copyrights, trademarks and patents are definitely other areas you want a lawyer and/or professional agent involved. There are time limits associated with each of these and it will depend on your application specifics, so be aware of yours and keep on top of this so that you stay protected.

Everything else essential for new business owners to know regarding legal matters and compliance has to do with corporate documents. Keeping up with them, the initial setup of your entity and the documents related to any changes are key to remaining compliant.

Important Documents

These are important to copy and have in a safe place within easy reach. You will need these items for business reasons and sometimes even for personal emergencies.

You can keep all of the items below in hard copy, if this is how you feel most comfortable, but there is something you should know…as you purchase services from other companies, these items are saved under secure passwords on the Internet, or on the 'cloud'.

The 'cloud' is just another way of saying 'online file' that only people with passwords you set or allow have access to. Every business does this. Every bank does this.

Every person providing most of the services a small business owner needs uses this type of secure service.

Why not get with a company that can help you create and control your own 'cloud file'? {At Pro Unum, we use a very secure service for organizing backup files on the cloud and helping them setup internal controls for legal vitals and financials. If you would like to learn more about us, CLICK HERE }

You should at least start to learn bit by bit how using this system and controlling access to it can help you stay disaster proof, even if you have hard copies at home.

Hard Copies to keep handy

EIN CP 575 letter that confirms your Tax Identification Number

Certificate from State Filing

Articles of organization or incorporation

Bylaws and Stock certificates

Any amendments made since initial filing

Business licenses, local registrations and permits

Any letter that came back from the IRS when you setup your company

Scanned backup on the 'cloud' (especially for owners and partners)

All of the above, and prior 5 years of tax returns (or at least the last 3 years)

Copy of current driver's license

Copy of Social Security Card and Birth Certificate (financial guarantor info of owners)

Insurance policies, certificates and card copies (bonds too, if applicable)

Bank Account Signature paperwork from the account opening meeting with banker

Summary

Summary

To conclude:

A little diligent effort each week can go a long way to make certain that you are on track for lower taxes and business success. By using systems like <u>QuickBooks</u>, Wave Accounting, or virtually any bookkeeping software available, you will be more up-to-date, more organized and more profitable all while saving lots of money you normally wouldn't on your taxes.

You will definitely catapult your small business further than most other small business owners in your industry, due to them not being this proactive and taking the time to handle these matters BEFORE they get out of control.

Help your business stay on point by doing the things that you will write out what you will pro-actively handle first on your checklists in the Maintenance section. You will see just how valuable all of this is when it is time to make big decisions about your business or your finances.

The time and money you will save every year because of your new diligent habits will give you more time to market, sell and grow your business…you know, doing the things you do best!

The numbers and notes you will have can literally get you lots of hours back to devoting your heart and soul to what you love doing in your business!

Learn more about how to put these things in motion the easy way by staying in contact with me and my private list. We will be holding entrepreneurial courses, giving great goodies away and helping each other stay up to date on all things small business (because let's face it folks, we've got to stick together!) Sign up for the Lagniappe Review today!

I will show you how effortless all of these tasks can be, show you how to avoid typical business owner problems (like years and years of backlogged bookkeeping or boxes upon boxes of messy receipts) that waste time and money and help you with a simplified work-flow that does all of these vital things for you.

And remember to get started with the sample checklist planners in the next section and help maintain tight control over what you pay in taxes from now on! You can download free copies of blank planners at my blog: www.natasharileynoah.com .

www.ingramcontent.com/pod-product-compliance
Lightning Source LLC
Chambersburg PA
CBHW081737170526

45167CB00009B/3845